EASTBOURNE
TO
HASTINGS

Vic Mitchell and Keith Smith

8800

Cover design – Deborah Goodridge

First published March 1986

ISBN 0 906520 27 4

© Middleton Press, 1986.

Typeset by CitySet · Bosham 573270

Published by Middleton Press
        Easebourne Lane
        Midhurst, West Sussex.
        GU29 9AZ
        073 081 3169

Printed & bound by Biddles Ltd
        Guildford and Kings Lynn.

CONTENTS

GEOGRAPHICAL SETTING

The horseshoe of chalk, the limbs of which are formed by the South Downs and the North Downs, contains a semi-circle of clay and a central block of sand or sandstone. Leaving Eastbourne, at the foot of the South Downs, the route crosses the end of the band of clay (submerged in Pevensey Levels and covered in shingle at the Crumbles) and reaches the first cutting through sand west of Bexhill. The final two miles of the route are largely in tunnels which pierce the tough sandstones of the Hastings Beds. This simplistic description overlooks the small outcrop of Tunbridge Wells Sand on which Pevensey stands.

All the maps in this album are to the scale of 25" to 1 mile, unless otherwise stated. (Railway Magazine)

ACKNOWLEDGEMENTS

Our grateful thanks go to all the photographers mentioned in the credits, many of whom have supplied much additional information. We also wish to thank Mrs E. Fisk, N. Stanyon and our wives for assistance with the text and N. Langridge for providing many of the tickets.

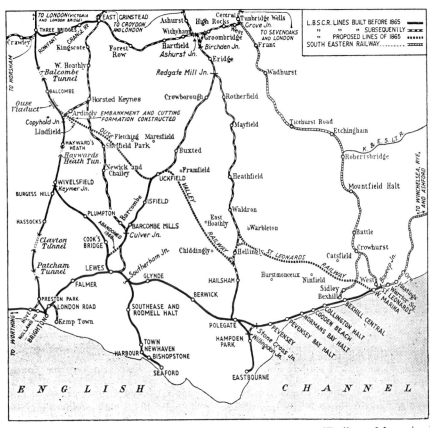

(Railway Magazine)

BRIGHTON AND SOUTH COAST RAILWAY

NEWHAVEN & DIEPPE ROUTE
TO ALL PARTS OF THE CONTINENT

SOUTHERN COUNTIES' CANINE ASSOCIATION
DOG SHOW
AT EGERTON PARK,
BEXHILL.

TUESDAY, JUNE 30th.

CHEAP DAY RETURN TICKETS
WILL BE ISSUED AS UNDER:—

BY TRAINS LEAVING AT			FROM	RETURN FARES To BEXHILL.			
				1st Class.		3rd Class.	
A.M.	A.M.	P.M.		s.	d.	s.	d.
9 33	10 30	1 0	HASTINGS	0	9	0	6
9 37	10 32	1 3	ST. LEONARDS (Warrior Square)	0	8	0	5
9 41	10 37	1 7	ST. LEONARDS (West Marina) ...	0	6	0	4
9 40	10 20	1 45	EASTBOURNE	1	10	1	4
10 28	11 57	1 51	LEWES	3	3	2	6
10 38	12 6 p.m.	2 34	GLYNDE	2	10	2	3
10 48	12 17	2 44	BERWICK	2	2	1	7
10 38	12 8	2 53	FOLEGATE	1	6	1	2
..	11 15 a.m.	1 49	HAMPDEN PARK ...	1	6	1	1
9 15	10 5	1 20	BRIGHTON (Central) ...	4	6	3	6
9 18	10 8	1 23	LONDON ROAD (Brighton) ...	4	4	3	3
9 31	...	2 3	PRESTON PARK	4	9	3	6
9 35	11 20	2 13	ROTHERFIELD	4	0	3	0
9 44	11 29	2 22	MAYFIELD	3	9	2	9
9 57	11 41	2 34	HEATHFIELD	3	2	2	6
10 6	11 50	2 43	WALDRON	2	10	2	0
10 15	11 59	2 51	HELLINGLY	2	3	1	8
10 20	12 4 p.m.	2 56	HAILSHAM ...	2	0	1	6
10 0	10 55 a.m.	1 50	TUNBRIDGE WELLS ...	4	0	3	0
10 6	11 4	1 58	GROOMBRIDGE	4	0	3	6
10 11	11 9	2 3	ERIDGE	4	0	3	0
10 19	...	2 24	CROWBOROUGH	4	6	3	0
10 29	...	2 35	BUXTED	4	6	3	0
10 34	...	2 44	UCKFIELD	4	6	3	0
10 40	...	2 50	ISFIELD	4	1	3	0
10 46	...	2 57	BARCOMBE MILLS ...	3	10	3	0
9 38	10 35	1 30	EAST GRINSTEAD	6	3	4	3
9 24	11 44	...	FOREST ROW	6	0	3	9
9 0	10 30	1 35	SEAFORD	4	7	3	6
9 4	10 34	2 34	BISHOPSTONE	4	5	3	3
9 9	10 37	1 40	NEWHAVEN HARBOUR ...	4	3	3	3
9 12	10 40	1 42	NEWHAVEN TOWN ...	4	2	3	3
9 34	11 31	...	PLUMPTON	4	1	3	0
9 43	11 38	...	COOKSBRIDGE ...	3	8	2	9
8 45	11 3	1 8	THREE BRIDGES ...	6	6	4	6
9 6	11 17	1 27	HAYWARDS HEATH ...	5	3	3	9
9 0	11 23	1 43	WIVELSFIELD	4	9	3	6
9 13	...	1 46	BURGESS HILL	4	9	3	6
9 19	...	1 51	HASSOCKS	4	9	3	6

TICKETS AVAILABLE FOR RETURN BY ANY TRAIN THE SAME DAY ONLY.
Passengers should ascertain if and where they have to change carriages.
CHEAP TICKETS are also issued to Bexhill by other Trains from some of the above-mentioned Stations. For Particulars see Cheap Ticket Programme.

NO LUGGAGE ALLOWED. CHILDREN OVER THREE AND UNDER TWELVE YEARS OF AGE, HALF-FARES.
The Railway Company give notice that tickets are issued subject to the conditions and regulations relating thereto and to the holders thereof set out in the Railway Company's Time Table Book.

HASTINGS AND ST. LEONARDS TICKETS can also be obtained at Mr. JOHN BRAY'S Railway and House Agency Offices, 13, South Colonnade, ST. LEONARDS.
TICKETS and other information can also be obtained at Messrs. PICKFORDS' Offices, 33, King's Road, St. Leonards; 4, Terminus Buildings, Terminus Road, Eastbourne; 46, Queen's Road, Brighton; also at Messrs. COOK & SON'S, 81, King's Road, Brighton.

London Bridge Terminus, June, 1914.   WILLIAM FORBES, General Manager.

HISTORICAL BACKGROUND

The first railway in the area was from the west, being an extension of the London, Brighton and South Coast Railway's line to Lewes, which had been opened in June 1846. It was opened through to Bulverhythe (west of St. Leonards) on 27th June of the same year.

The second line in the district was from the east, being a branch of the South Eastern Railway's main line at Ashford. This reached Hastings in 1851 and the SER was responsible for the construction of a line through two tunnels to link up with the LBSCR and its own direct route to London (via Battle) at Bopeep Junction. Services commenced on 13th February 1851 but because of hostility between the two companies, LBSCR trains were halted the next day. Tension eased and services resumed the following day but during the next night SER workmen tore up track near the junction, barricaded the line and impounded two LBSCR locomotives and some rolling stock at Hastings. The LBSCR decided to operate a bus service but the SER retaliated by quickly erecting gates at the end of the road to the station! It was not until 26th February that a Court order brought the farce to an end. The following year saw the opening of the SER's direct line to London and an agreement made with the LBSCR for the sharing of receipts at Hastings station.

A branch line service commenced operation between Polegate and Eastbourne on 14th May 1849 but it was not until 2nd August 1871 that a triangular junction was formed to allow direct running between Hastings and Eastbourne. The original branch was single track, which was doubled in 1862.

A notable event in the history of the route was the introduction of electric traction on 7th July 1935 which further stimulated the growth of tourism and residential development in the area.

PASSENGER SERVICES

Initially five weekday trains were provided, with two on Sundays, between Brighton and St. Leonards (Bulverhythe). In 1869, there were six services on weekdays (two on Sundays) between Lewes and Hastings, with connections at Polegate for Eastbourne. By 1890 the direct services had been increased to nine with five more running via Eastbourne and two terminating there.

A railmotor service between Eastbourne and St. Leonards West Marina commenced on 14th September 1905, calling at a number of new halts. There were six return journeys daily, for third class passengers only. This was reduced to three, with one trip east as far as Pevensey, in 1910.

In addition to the railmotors, the 1910 timetable provided 17 trains each way along the coast line, of which six ran into Eastbourne. By the mid-1920s there were 27 journeys, 15 of which went into Eastbourne.

Electrification in 1935 provided a basic service of two stopping trains an hour between Brighton and Ore and an hourly fast between Victoria and Ore, all running via Eastbourne.

Through trains from the Midlands and North of England featured in the summer timetables between the Wars and were particularly well patronised at week-ends in the 1950s. They were withdrawn in 1963.

Less well known were the through trains along the South Coast, such as the Brighton to Margate service of the Edwardian era.

The present basic service gives an hourly fast train between Hastings and Victoria with an all-stations service between Hastings and Brighton, the latter not operating in times of low demand.

The additional services between St. Leonards and Hastings on the Tonbridge route will be described in a later album.

EASTBOURNE

1. This must be one of the oldest of Eastbourne's railway photographs. It was taken in March 1881, but unfortunately the plate quality has suffered since. The locomotive was built as no.214 in 1865 and scrapped in 1882, bearing no.369. Details worth looking for include a top hat, wooden scaffold poles and a passenger communication gong. (E.R. Lacey collection)

3. To read the advertisements shown in this postcard view, is to gain a little insight into customs and prices of the day. (Lens of Sutton)

EASTBOURNE.

THE . . .

EASTBOURNE

ROYAL RESTAURANT.

VISITORS spending

A DAY IN EASTBOURNE

will find that the Royal Restaurant in the Terminus Road has been entirely reconstructed and furnished throughout in the most luxuriant style.

56a, TERMINUS ROAD.

2. The town is fortunate in having the elegance of its Victorian terminus largely unspoilt. The first station was a timber structure built on the site of the present Post Office and was replaced by a temporary one in 1866, north of Upperton Road. This in turn was replaced by the present one in 1872, which was extensively enlarged and rebuilt in 1886. The bath chair, the open-top omnibus and bare-back horse add atmosphere to this view from Terminus Road. (Lens of Sutton)

4. No doubt this photograph was taken to feature the well groomed class E4 no.488 and not the accident in the background. The short wheelbase horse box is another incidental item of interest. (E.R. Lacey collection)

5. The signal gantry by the locomotive shed carries four pairs of signals. The lower ones are not true distant signals but were used to indicate whether the lines were clear through to the buffers or if the platform was partly obstructed by vans or horse boxes for example. Only the signal box survives today. (Lens of Sutton)

6. Another photograph of signal interest. The posts are wider near the arms and also slotted so that the pivot is within the post. The lamps are remote from the arms and rotate to show change of aspect. There is also a good view of a loading gauge of the period and some privately owned coal wagons. (Lens of Sutton)

LONDON, EASTBOURNE, ST. LEONARDS, and HASTINGS.—London, Brighton, and South Coast.

Week Days.

Down.

		mrn	**m**	mrn	mrn	non	aft	aft		**D**		**m**	aft	aft	aft	**n**	aft	aft	aft	aft	aft
Victoria	dep.		9 45	...	1115	12 0	1 25	...				3 20	...	4 30	...	5 20	5 45	6 45	...	7 40	9 50
Kensington †	"		9 33	...		1140	1240	...				3 35	...		...		6 35	...	7 17	9 25	
Clapham Junction	"		9 52		12 7	1 32	...							5s50	6 52	...	7 47	9 57		
London Bridge	"	6 20	9 59	53	1150	1c27	2 0	...				4 5	5 5	...		7 07	459	13	...
New Cross	"	...	40 1		1151	1 16	...					3 36			...	6 52	...	9 0	...
East Croydon	"	6 39	1010	1021		1227	1 52	19				4 24	24	...		7 87	2 8	8 1016	
EASTBOURNE	arr.	8 7	1135	1238	1245	2 23	2 63	52			4 4	4 55	6 05	50 6	18	6 35	6 50	7 35	8 34	9 129	45	1150
BEXHILL	"	8 23	1145	5	2 29	3 37	3 57		4 9	5 5	6 9	7 37	3 8	39 9	26	1214	
ST. LEONARDS*	"	8 32	1152	12	2 37	45	4	4 16	5 11	6 16	7 107	10	8 46	9 34	1222	
"	"	8 37	1157	16	2 42	51	4 10	4 21	5 16	6 22	7 157	15	8 51	9 39	r	
HASTINGS	"	8 40	12 01	20	2 45	55	4 14	4 25	5 20	6 25	7 187	18	8 55	9 43	1230	

Up.

		mrn	mrn	mrn	mrn	mrn	**i**	mrn	mrn	mrn		mrn	**i**	aft	aft	aft	aft	aft	aft		
HASTINGS	dep.	6 0	6 50	7 45	8 15	8 25	...	1022	1046		1150		2 10	...	5 10	7 25	...	9 50		
ST. LEONARDS‡	"	6 36	27	48	8 18	28	...	1024	1043		1153		2 14	...	5 13	7 28	...	9 33		
"	"	6 7	6 56	7 52	8 22	33	...	1028	1047	11a5	1157		2 19	...	5 18	7 32	...	9 37		
BEXHILL	"	6 14	7 47	59	8 30	8 41	...	1035	1054	1113a		12 5		2 29	...	5 26	7 39	...	9 45	
EASTBOURNE	"	6 25	7 10	8 6	30	...	9 30	1046	1135	1155		12102	26	...	4 35	5 30	7 45	8 30	9 45	
East Croydon	arr.	8 32	8 54	9 47	47	...	1038	1042	1222	28		1 58	2 53	4	1 26	1 07	1 79	46	1023	1222
New Cross	"	...					1 0			2 13	5	4	...	7 35	10 4	1038	1240	
London Bridge	"	8 50	9 15	10	1015	1052	11 3	1243			2 20	1	54	26	30 7	43	1010	1047	1247
Clapham Junction	"	9 49	731	10 3	...	1057		1248			2 10	1	8	27 6	25 7	38	10 3	...	1242
Kensington †	"	9 26	9 59	1021	...	1122		1258	1 54		2 35	1	4 23	4	54 6	55 8	26	1019	...
Victoria	"	9 12	9 22	1013	...	11 5	11 0	1248		1 30		2 2	1	4 17	35 6	33 7	48	1012	1050	1252

NOTES.

a Motor Car, one class only.
b Pullman Car to London Bridge.
c Leaves at 1 15 aft. on Saturdays.
i Pullman Car to Victoria.
l Slip Carriage.
m Pullman Car, Victoria to Eastbourne.
n Pullman Car to Eastbourne, except Sats.
p Pullman Car to Eastbourne.
r Sets down.
s Saturdays only.
* West Marina.
† Addison Road.
‡ Warrior Square.

1910

7. The turntable had to be used to gain access to any one of the eight shed roads. The locomotive is a Craven goods engine no. 390, built in 1866, photographed here in about 1887 and scrapped in 1896.
(E.R. Lacey collection)

1900 map to 6″ to 1 mile. More detailed maps and other photographs appear in our *Brighton to Eastbourne* album.

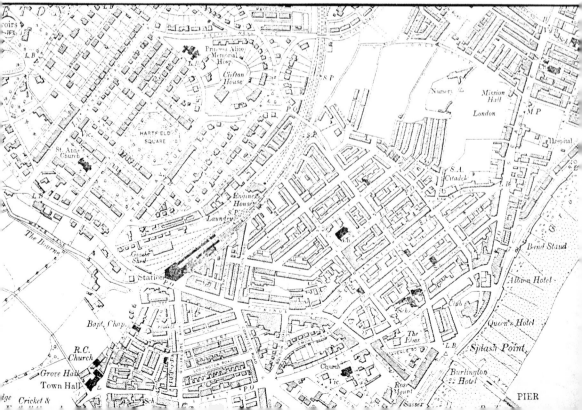

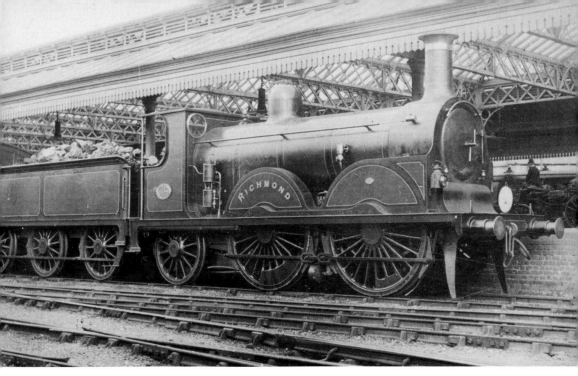

8. A feature of the station not seen in other photographs is the covered cab road. No. 608 *Richmond* gives a tidy appearance with its inside bearings and motion, particularly as it has stopped so that its coupling rod is hidden by the framing. (E.R. Lacey collection)

9. The large roof (left of centre) is that of the semi-roundhouse engine shed, closed in 1911. The siding in the foreground passed under Cavendish Place in a separate bridge to the main line and reached the Duke of Devonshire's Estate Yard. It could take 20 wagons in contrast to the single wagon siding on the extreme left of the picture. This was to the Carrara Wharf of R. Francis & Sons, monumental masons. The deflections in the fence brought about by these two gates can be seen to this day. (Lens of Sutton)

10. In 1905, two steam railmotors and two petrol-driven cars were purchased. The petrol cars were originally provided with gangways so that they could be used in tandem. This view shows one of them after rebuilding with enclosed ends. Another view of this forerunner of the Sprinter class 150 DMU is shown in picture no.89.
(R.C. Riley collection)

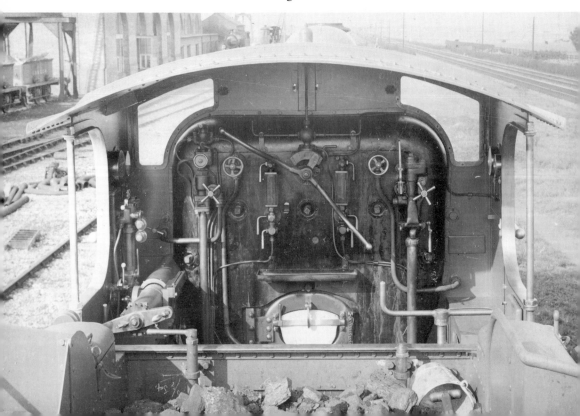

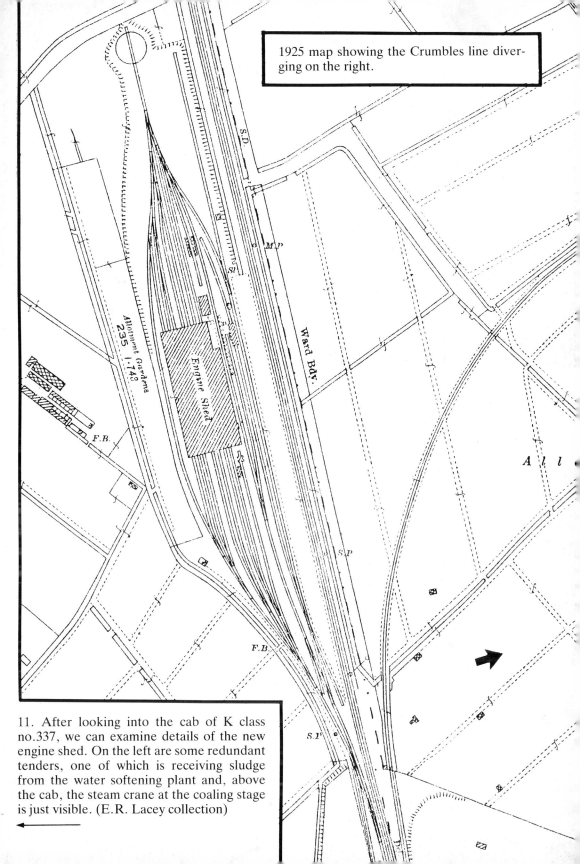

1925 map showing the Crumbles line diverging on the right.

Allotment Gardens
235 1·74²

Engine Shed

F.B.

S.D

M.P

S.P

Ward Bdy.

A l l

S.P

F.B.

S.P

11. After looking into the cab of K class no.337, we can examine details of the new engine shed. On the left are some redundant tenders, one of which is receiving sludge from the water softening plant and, above the cab, the steam crane at the coaling stage is just visible. (E.R. Lacey collection)

12. An interesting experiment started in 1929 at the north end of the shed. U class no. A629 was converted to burn pulverised coal, a fuel now widely used in power stations, and a special plant was erected over no.1 road. Ex-SECR Terrier no.751 provided the steam for it. It is seen here with wooden brake blocks, no coupling rods and an Ashford boiler. It had been built as no.54 *Waddon* and survived with BR until 1962, when it retired to Montreal. The fine coal dust necessitated a cover on the tender and caused a serious explosion in 1932, which terminated the experiment. Black dust rained down on the town, producing numerous complaints and Brand X washing on the clothes lines. (H.F. Wheeller)

13. Although of little strategic importance, the town suffered badly from air raids in WWII. Platforms 1 and 2 were damaged on 4th May 1942 and again in 1944. In the background is the sizeable goods shed. (British Rail)

14. Another raid in 1942, on 16th September, caused extensive damage. Only a few minutes' flying time from enemy airfields, the bombs were sometimes dropped before the siren warning sounded. Inland there was usually several minutes warning. (British Rail)

15. Even after the electrification of coastal services in 1935, there was plenty to delight steam enthusiasts. This fine study in light and shade was taken on 6th November 1949 and the train was the 10.16am to Tunbridge Wells. The locomotive is class I3 no.32081. (S.C. Nash)

LOCAL PARCEL : PAID.

London Brighton & South Coast Rly.
122 (57A)

TO

ST. LEONARDS (MARINA)

FROM WORTHING

16. Another class I3, no.32077, with the 10.45am Hastings to Birmingham New Street on 1st July 1950. The train reversed and changed locomotives at both Eastbourne and Brighton. The Crumbles line is on the right, with the turnout to the Bainbridge and Shell-Mex siding in the middle distance. The East-bourne Corporation siding and the former waterworks is beyond the fence on the left. (S.C. Nash)

17. In June 1951, an exhibition was held of rolling stock and equipment forming part of the Modernisation Programme. Included in the show were 4–6–0s nos. 73001 and 75000; Pacific no. 70009 *Alfred the Great*; electric locomotive no. 20003 (then only 2 years old); diesel locomotive no. 10100 (the "Fell") and shunter no. 15227. (S.C. Nash)

18. The dereliction of the shed by 1955 is evident in this view of the north end. It seems that after the 1935 electrification scheme, the inspection pits and smoke ducts were removed from nos. 4 to 7 roads, to reduce the rating assessment. The roof was extensively damaged by bombs and subsequently removed piecemeal. The shed had been opened in 1911 and was closed to steam in June 1965. It was used for stabling diesels until 1968 and was demolished in the following year. (S.C. Nash)

19. On 25th August 1958, the 7.45pm Glasgow to Eastbourne car sleeper train collided with the 6.47am Ore to London Bridge train, the 12 coaches of which were standing in the platform. The second coach was telescoped – the leading coach (no.11027) is being lifted clear by the Brighton crane – the signal gantry has come down – a railway operator's nightmare. (British Rail)

21. Whilst D2282 shunts coal wagons in the loco shed sidings, class 4 no.80138 heads north with the Hastings coaches of an overnight train from Manchester on 27th July 1963. What a way to start your holiday! (S.C. Nash)

20. The car sleeper was hauled by no.73042 which is seen here on the day after the accident, standing outside the shed. There were five fatalities and 25 passengers injured in the tragedy. (C.J. Hughes)

This 1910 map continues north from the map opposite picture no.111 in our *Brighton to Eastbourne* album. It shows a number of industrial sidings to the east of the main line. Parallel to this is the Crumbles line, from which branches Bainbridge's siding. Next comes Davey & Mannington's timber siding. The extensive coal yard is between Whitley Road Bridge and Cavendish Bridge and, at the bottom, the line into the Duke of Devonshire's Estate Yard.

St. Philip's

Pumping Station
(Eastbourne Water Wks. Co.)

Timber Yd.

F.F.

F.F.

R.H.

MAYFIELD PLACE

L L R O A D

UPPER AVENUE

A V E N U E

U P E R A V E N U E

UPPER AVENUE

S.R. Coal Depot

WINTER ROAD

DENNIS ROAD

PR

22. LMR no. 45102 accelerates past the waterworks on 20th June 1964, with empty stock bound for Willesden. The waterworks had ceased to be used as such in about 1925, owing to pollution of the well. (S.C. Nash)

23. Although photographed in 1976, the signal box is little changed at the time of writing, 10 years later, and it is now one of the largest mechanical boxes in the south of England. The multi-storey car park in the background is a good vantage point for the railway observer. (J. Scrace)

24. After a day enjoying the seaside delights of the town, excursionists return to Barnsley in a rake of ageing Mk.I coaches, hauled by no. 47174 on Easter Monday 1976. (S.C. Nash)

26. Excursions, although less frequent, still make this pleasant town their destination. On Easter Sunday 1984, this train from Wolverhampton had taken an unusual route via Ashford and Hastings. No. 33033 runs in, past the site of the former carriage sidings between platforms 2 and 3. (J.S. Petley)

London Brighton & South Coast Railway.

Littlehampton to

Hastings

25. The South Downs seen in the background are another holiday attraction, especially where they terminate at the cliffs of Beachy Head. The truncated train is the empty newspaper train returning to London on Easter Sunday 1982, behind no. 73185. In 1983, the sidings were rationalised and two carriage washing plants were erected. A short siding was provided for Corralls oil depot. (J.S. Petley)

THE CRUMBLES

27. The coast between Eastbourne and Pevensey is composed of a massive shingle bank, up to ¾ mile wide, known as The Crumbles. Totally infertile, the only use for the area was for the location of a Victorian isolation hospital for infectious diseases and for supplying ballast to the LBSCR. For the latter purpose, a branch nearly three miles long was laid in about 1862. The unfenced "tramway" was an ideal location for official photographs to be taken, such as this one of the *Southern Belle* Pullman stock in 1908, before its introduction between London and Brighton. No.19 was of the unsuccessful class I2s, best suited for moving a train on level ground and certainly not to London.
(E.R. Lacey collection)

28. The last day of regular steam operation of the line was 30th April 1960 and class E4 no.32468 approaches Ringwood Road level crossing. Diesel class 03 or 04 was provided until 08s arrived in August 1965. (S.C. Nash)

29. In 1926 a ½ mile branch from the main branch was opened to the Corporation's Electric Light Works, although the latter had been built in 1902. The line not only carried coal to the works (up to 10,000 tons per annum) but also petrol to the Corporation's bus garage and scrap metal away from the Refuse Destructor Works. Traffic ceased in February 1967 and two years later only this electrically powered crane remained on isolated track. It was built by the Bedford Engineering Co. and could shunt wagons at a tortoise pace. (S.C. Nash)

30. Class E1 tanks operated the branch in the Edwardian era, followed by the class E2, which ran until about 1925. These were followed by class E3 0–6–2Ts which were in turn replaced in 1935 by class E4s, helped sometimes by E5s. The C2X and A1X classes were not unknown. Here E4 no. 32518, creeps along near Churchdale Road in about 1950, when a 5mph speed restriction was imposed, due to weak bridges. (J.J. Smith)

31. In 1985 part of the dismantled rail route formed a footpath through Bridgemere Estate. Here we look westwards, just west of the site of Churchdale Road level crossing. Until 1950, the line was officially known as "Gas Works & Ballast Hole Single Line" and thereafter simply as "Down Siding". (S.C. Nash)

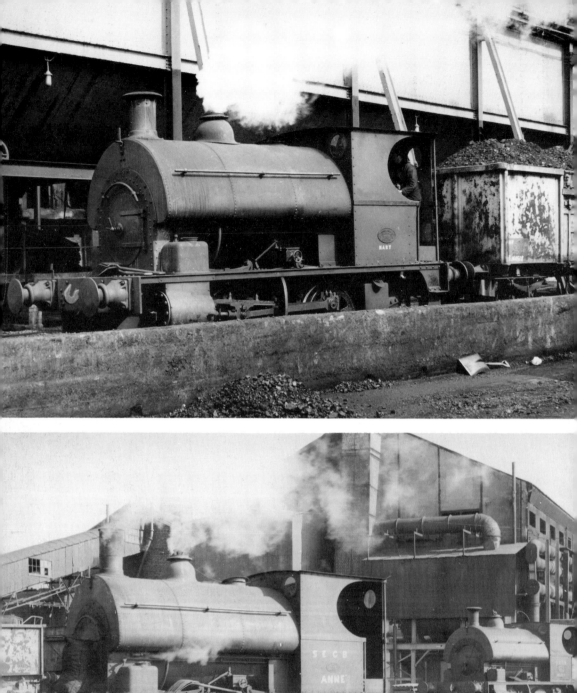

32. In 1870 the Eastbourne Gas Company decided to build a new works to the east of the town. The direction of the prevailing wind would dissipate the sulphurous odours and a goods branch line already existed. The works straddled the railway and required up to 40,000 tons of coal each year. It produced coke as a by-product which was taken by rail to Eastbourne. *Mary* was built by Avonside in 1909. (S.C. Nash)

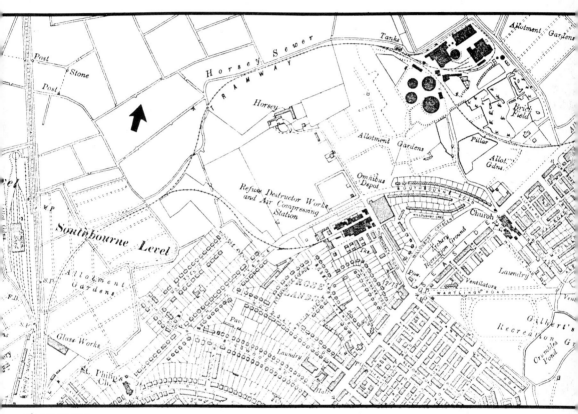

33. The closure of the works in 1967 deprived the branch of its last regular traffic, the last load of coal from Newhaven arriving on 28th March. *Anne* was built in 1914 by the same manufacturer as her sister. A siding near the gas works had once been provided for manure to be unloaded for the allotments. (S.C. Nash)

The 1930 6″ scale map fails to name the gas works (top right) or the electricity works (centre and adjacent to the destructor works). The line to the "ballast hole" is on the right.

34. Both locomotives had been transferred from Sydenham Gas Works – *Anne* in 1958 and *Mary* in 1964 – and were both scrapped in 1968. There were many other cases of the locomotive shed supporting a water tank. (S.C. Nash)

35. The Turnpike Road was renamed Seaside before 1900 and is now the A259. By 1932 the line east of the level crossing was disused and buffers were erected. These can be seen in September 1950, behind the road sign which refers to Lothbridge Drove, the lane to Hampden Park, now a major road. A round-about is now provided at this turning. (E.C. Griffith)

36. The boarded crossing keeper's cottage survived until the road was widened, not long after this photograph was taken in August 1955. Sidings had earlier served the timber merchants' yard and probably a small brickworks, both west of the crossing.
(E.C. Griffith)

Extract from the 1934 working instructions. "Turnpike Road" should have read "Seaside" and "Southbourne Road" was in fact "St. Phillips Avenue".

Continued overleaf →

Gas Works and Ballast Hole single line.—This single line is a continuation of the down siding and commences at a point immediately south of Whitley Road overline bridge.

No train must enter upon the single line unless the Driver is in the possession of the train staff on which is engraved the words "Gas Works and Ballast Hole Line." The Signalman on duty at Eastbourne signal box is responsible for handing the train staff to the Driver before allowing a movement to be made on the single line, and the Driver must return it to the Signalman when the train returns from the single line.

The following sidings are connected with the single line in the order shown, commencing at the Eastbourne end :—

Davey & Mannington and Lunsford & Co. siding ; Bainbridge and Shell Mex Ltd. sidings ; Eastbourne Corporation Electricity Works siding ; Eastbourne Gas Works siding ; Lewis Gasson's siding ; and Ballast Hole.

Davey & Mannington and Lunsford & Co.'s siding is fitted with Annett's patent lock, the key being fitted to the train staff.

Ballast trains, engines, etc., must pass through the Gas Works siding at a speed not exceeding 5 miles per hour, and sound the engine whistle on approaching.

Great care must be exercised in crossing the Turnpike Road to and from the Ballast Hole ; Drivers, Guards and Shunters must keep a good look-out for road traffic, and the engine whistle must be sounded on approaching the road in both directions.

37. The chestnut fencing on the left was seen in the previous view, around the crossing keeper's garden. This May 1950 eastward view shows the British Petroleum sidings (disused for nearly 20 years) and a row of trolleys, ready for the demolition gang. (J.J. Smith)

Continued from overleaf.

The Eastbourne Corporation Electricity Works siding is situate about 774 yards from Messrs. Bainbridge and Shell Mex Ltd. sidings. The hand points giving access to the siding are facing for movements approaching from the direction of Eastbourne, and must be set normally for the Ballast Hole line. Catch points are provided at the entrance to the siding and also on the eastern side of the Southbourne Road level crossing gates. The Southbourne Road level crossing and Roselands Avenue level crossing are protected by gates and before shunting operations in the siding are commenced, the Guard, or Shunter in charge, must satisfy himself that the Eastbourne Corporation Electricity Works have provided a man to operate the gates during the time shunting operations are in progress. The Driver must sound the whistle on entering the siding, as an indication to the man operating the gates and be prepared to bring the movement to a stand clear of the gates, if necessary. Inwards traffic will be propelled into the siding and placed on one line of the loop, and outwards traffic taken from the other line of the loop and hauled from the siding. The Company's engine must not proceed beyond the hand points on the eastern side of the loop line. No wagon or load exceeding 10 feet in height above rail level, or 9 feet over-all width, is allowed beyond the restriction board erected on the gantry brickwork situated at the western end of the Corporation dust destructor. The Guard, or Shunter in charge, will be responsible for seeing that vehicles left in the siding are properly secured.

Gates are provided at entrances to sidings and at various other places on the single line, and Drivers must stop at each gate for the Guard to alight and open it, and again after the train or engine has passed through, for the gate to be closed.

When returning from the single line and the fixed signal is lowered, the Driver must stop before reaching the coal yard points, and the Guard or Shunter in charge must satisfy himself that the trailing points are properly set and give a hand signal to the Driver accordingly.

38. In 1931, the Duke of Devonshire leased the shingle extraction rights to Hall & Co. Until that time, up to a dozen wagons of ballast had been taken daily to the estate siding seen previously in picture no.9. The SR chose the harder granite ballast from Meldon Quarry in Devon and ceased to use the more rounded marine-worn material from the Crumbles. Hall & Co's Hunslet no.46 is shown in use in 1955. (E.C. Griffith)

39. Hall & Co also used the Simplex on their 2ft. gauge system which was about a mile long. This 1950 westward shot shows the standard gauge trackbed, east of Wallis Avenue, and the method of winning the ballast. Another unusual chapter of railway history has ended as urban development spreads over these once desolate wastes. (S.C. Nash)

40. Modern Electric Tramways Ltd was founded by Mr Claude W. Lane and commenced operating miniature tramcars at Eastbourne in July 1954 on 2ft gauge track, having previously run a 15″ gauge line in Rhyl. Car no.3 was the third tram to be built and was to a 1903 design. (S.C. Nash)

41. No.226 was similar to Mr Lane's second tram no.225, both being models of Blackpool tramcars of those numbers. Both these photographs were taken at the eastern end of

42. Car no.2 was built at the company's Eastbourne workshops to resemble the former Metropolitan Tramway vehicles. The seats, controllers and gongs were genuine tram components. One terminus was at Royal Parade, but this car is going in the opposite direction, the driver having forgotten to change the blind. (S.C. Nash)

the line in August 1954. A further extension in 1958 brought the route distance to nearly one mile. (S.C. Nash)

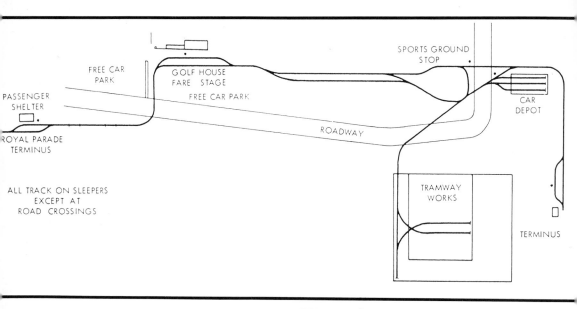

FREE CAR
PARK

GOLF HOUSE
FARE STAGE

FREE CAR PARK

SPORTS GROUND
STOP

PASSENGER
SHELTER

ROADWAY

CAR
DEPOT

ROYAL PARADE
TERMINUS

ALL TRACK ON SLEEPERS
EXCEPT AT
ROAD CROSSINGS

TRAMWAY
WORKS

TERMINUS

43. The same car is accelerating away after having stopped at the Golf House, one of the passing places. Even the overhead structures had an Emett flavour. Power was supplied by the company's own 60 volt DC generators. (S.C. Nash)

44. No.7 was built in 1958 and was over 22ft long and 4ft wide, seating 40 people. The line commenced at the junction of Channel View Road and Royal Parade and passed through Princes Park to reach the Golf House, prior to running onto the Crumbles. (S.C. Nash)

45. Unfortunately animosity arose between the Corporation and the company over financial matters, the latter deciding that a new operating site was desirable. All the equipment was moved to Devon and a tramway of 2'9" gauge was laid out on the trackbed of the former branch line to Seaton, opening on 27th August 1970. This and the previous five photographs were taken twelve months earlier. (S.C. Nash)

46. Devoid of smoke deflectors, class U1 no.1902 brakes a stopping train from Brighton on 23rd October 1934. Willingdon was the original name of the station, which was opened on 1st January 1888. It was renamed on 1st July 1903. (H.C. Casserley)

1910 map

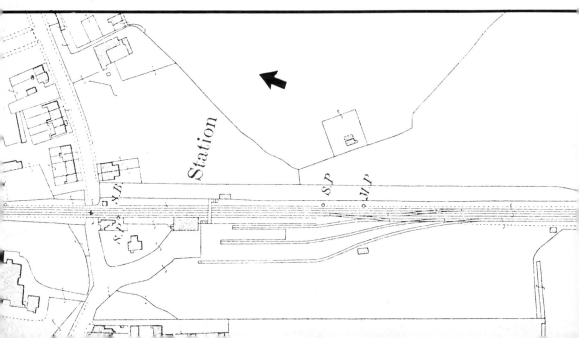

47. Extra passenger traffic at holiday times often necessitated the use of goods engines, such as Q class no.30534 on Maundy Thursday in 1949. This train was the 4.02pm relief from Victoria and had run via Heathfield, to reduce congestion on the main line. In the foreground is the goods yard headshunt which was still in place in 1985, although unusued. (S.C. Nash)

48. With gas lamps still in evidence, an N class 2–6–0 waits with a train bound for Tonbridge via Heathfield and Eridge. Many of the station's features were similar to those at Fittleworth. (E. Wilmshurst)

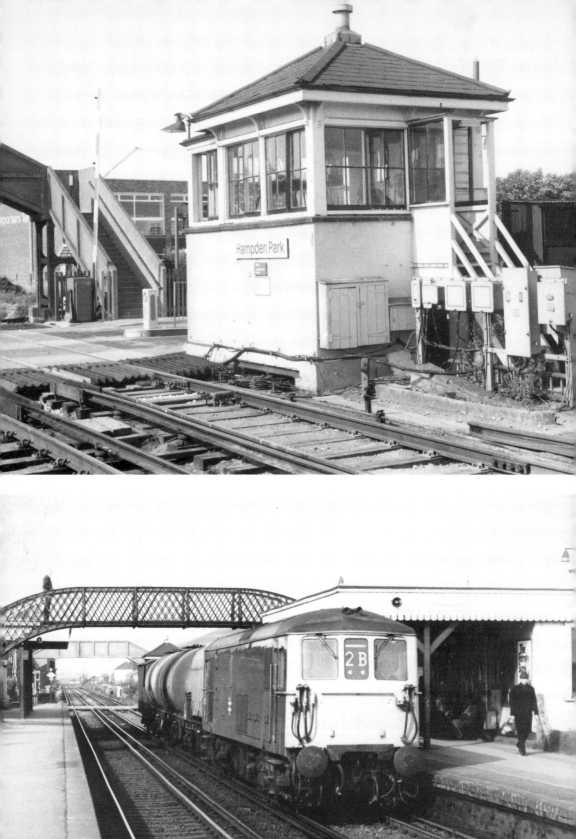

49. Lifting barriers replaced the level crossing gates on 5th April 1976 and a flat-roofed extension was added to the north side of the box. The goods yard at the opposite end of the station was closed on 30th November 1964. (J. Scrace)

51. Half a mile north of the station is Willingdon Junction which until 1930 had its own signal box. In March 1985, no.73137 passes over the unworked trailing points of the down junction, the up junction being worked from Hampden Park. (S.C. Nash)

London Brighton & South Coast Railway.

Rotherfield to

Hampden Park

50. On 2nd March 1982, the 14.03 St. Leonards to Brighton freight had shrunk somewhat. Behind no.73133 is a lattice steel footbridge intended for ticket holders and in the background is a concrete bridge for pedestrians unwilling to wait at the barriers. (J.S. Petley)

STONE CROSS

52. The windmill in the background is just east of Stone Cross, close to the A27. The train is a Saga Charter from Newcastle on 12th June 1983 and is rounding the curve that was once the eastern part of the triangular junction. No.33020 had brought the special via Ashford and Hastings. (J.S. Petley)

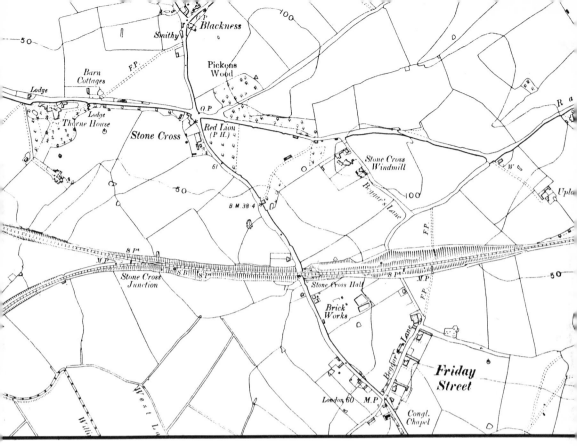

1910 six inch scale map

53. On the northern part of the triangle, we see K class no.32350 hauling empty coaches from Polegate to Hastings on 15th August 1959 with Lower Willingdon and the South Downs in the background. This line was formally closed on 6th January 1969 but was used by occasional works trains until 1974. One track remained as an engineer's siding from Stone Cross Junction for a further 10 years. (J.J. Smith)

54. The halt was erected in 1905 and remained in use for 30 years, being served by rail motors. Class B4 no.2054 runs through on 9th October 1933, with the junction signals in the background. (H.C. Casserley)

55. Opened as Westham & Pevensey, the station is close to the centre of Westham and about one mile from Pevensey. The tiny goods shed was a feature of many LBSCR rural stations as were the milk churns and the horse and cart. (Lens of Sutton) 1927

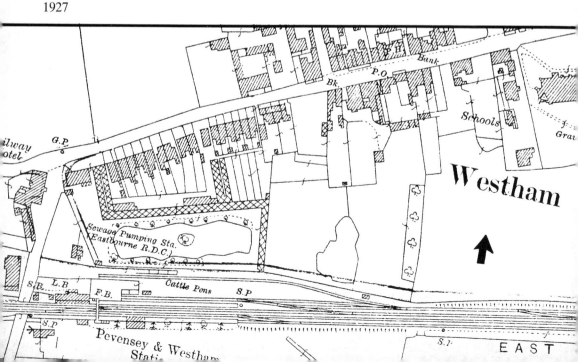

56. An October 1933 shot reveals two cattle wagons on the rear of the two coach train, hauled by class D1 0–4–2T no.2254. South of the station are the Mountney Levels, reclaimed land leading to the Crumbles. (H.C. Casserley)

57. By November 1948, the tall tapered wooden signal post, seen in the previous photograph, had been greatly shortened and was eventually replaced by one made from two former running rails. Class C2X no.2434 blows off, whilst retarding its mixed freight bound for St. Leonards. (J.J. Smith)

58. During the lengthy ASLEF strike in 1955, some unusual trains were operated by NUR crews. This is the 4.05pm Three Bridges to Hastings service on 6th June, hauled by LM 2–6–2T no.41317. Much freight traffic was permanently lost to road haulage – this goods yard closed in 1961. (S.C. Nash)

59. Ageing electric trains have their admirers. 2BIL set no.2090 is in the care of the National Railway Museum and 4SUB no.4732, behind it, is still owned by BR. The headboard indicates the railtour organisers and the date. (C. Wilson)

London Brighton & South Coast Railway.

Pevensey & Westham to

Hellingly

60. The north facade of the station still gives the impression of a country station unchanged for decades. Few have retained a canopy on both sides of the building. (Janet Smith)

61. Another 1985 view shows the many features to have remained unchanged on the down side. Whilst semaphore signalling is retained, the up platform has only a bus shelter and the road has been protected by barriers since 1975. (Janet Smith)

PEVENSEY BAY

62. This is the second halt on the route to be built for the railmotor service in 1905. It did not take its name from the existing signal box but was given one with tourism in mind. The barriers were installed in 1974 and controlled from Pevensey & Westham box from May 1976. (S.C. Nash)

63. On 28th September 1984, both off side barriers failed to lower on the approach of the 12.30 Hastings to Victoria. The train is seen here stationary, with the driver re-entering his cab after the barriers had been operated manually. (C. Wilson)

London Brighton & South Coast Railway.

Lewes to

Ramsgate

S. E. R., via HASTINGS.

64. Pevensey Castle, with its third century origin, would have attracted Edwardian travellers to alight at the short wooden rail- motor platform. Present day tourists to the lengthy concrete structure are few in number. (Janet Smith)

NORMANS BAY

65. In October 1934 the halt retained its timber platform and oil lights. Class F1 no.1060 chases through with a train from Hastings. Grassed-over sand dunes and a Martello tower are the only notable features of the landscape. (H.C. Casserley)

COODEN BEACH

66. The 1905 station naming committee chose to ignore the local name of Pevensey Sluice, presumably because of its association with bedpans. Nearly 80 years later the newly electrified *Bed*ford - St. *Pan*cras route actually became known as the Bedpan line. How tastes change. The 4CIG is about to pass over Havensmouth level crossing, another case of a halt having a name different from the associated crossing. (C. Wilson)

67. Known variously as Cooden Golf and Cooden Halt it has now assumed the status of a station, although the signal box was plain Cooden, as seen in this 1921 official photograph. (British Rail)

68. On the left are some of the signals controlled by Cooden Box and the path leading down from the halt whilst on the right a tram departs from its terminus. (R. Resch collection)

69. Looking north from the tram terminus, we can see the method of construction of the halt which appears to have been extended on the left. The SR later undertook a major rebuild, mainly in concrete, as nearby residential development increased the passenger traffic. (Hastings Reference Library)

70. Few waiting passengers would be aware of the contents of the vans behind this ageing eastbound M7. They contained the costumes, scenery and props of a travelling theatrical company. Many such specials were still run when this photograph was taken in May 1956. (J.J. Smith)

71. The concrete lighting standards, platform slabs and fencing panels were typical products of the SR's concrete works at Exmouth Junction between the World Wars. Hexagonal lampshades were another standard SR design. (D. Cullum collection)

72. The 1935 austere but functional exterior gave no direct indication of its purpose, in 1985. Having crossed Hooe Level, the route from this station onwards is almost entirely in the urbanised area that joins up with Hastings. (Janet Smith)

73. When the motor train service commenced in 1905 the halt was named Collington Wood but was soon closed only to be reopened as West Bexhill Halt on 1st September 1911. This was changed to Collington Halt in December 1929, the 'halt' being dropped by BR in 1970. This photograph was taken in 1921 to show the then new Braggs Lane footbridge. (British Rail)

London Brighton & South Coast Railway.

Hastings to

HAMPDEN PARK

74. Petrol and steam railmotors initiated the service to the halts but were of limited success, being replaced by push and pull sets, such as this one proceeding towards Hastings, in the charge of class D1 no.2699. (Lens of Sutton)

75. The first station was situated in open country on a site that was later to become the goods yard and is now a car park, south of the Town Hall. This photograph is thought to date from about 1868 and shows the station's only signal post, which had one arm for each direction. The signalman is standing in front of his cabin with his hand on one of the two levers. (R.C. Riley collection)

BEXHILL

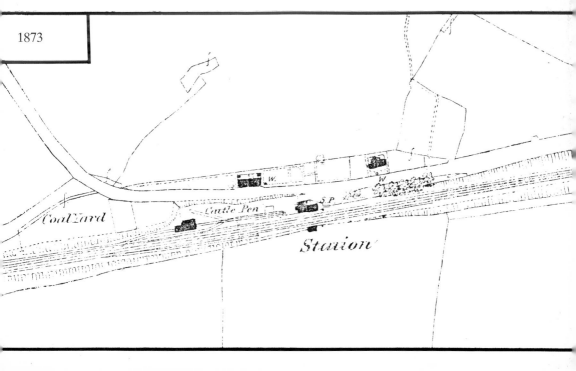

1873

CENTRAL STATION, BEXHILL-ON-SEA

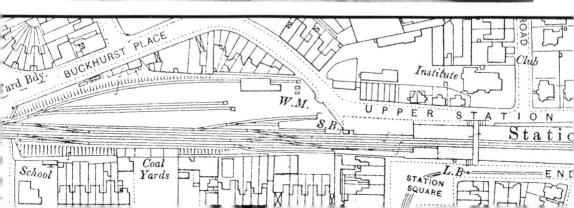

76. This view shows the generous platform width allowed for passengers in the 1902 rebuilding. The population had multiplied five times in the previous 20 years and so provision for expansion was justified. Railmotor no.2 had a boiler of 3′6″ diameter *and* length. It appears fairly new in this view. (R.C. Riley collection)

78. Local football clubs once required special trains on winter Saturdays. This is the empty stock of a Hailsham to Bexhill special, being taken back to Eastbourne on 2nd April 1955. On the right is an end-loading dock, once used by Hall & Co. (S.C. Nash)

77. The station was given the suffix 'Central' on 9th July 1923 by the SR, to distinguish it from the former SECR station, which it designated 'West'. The elegant lantern roof and the front canopy survive today. (Lens of Sutton)

The 1909 map shows double tram track outside the station merging to a single line in Endwell Road.

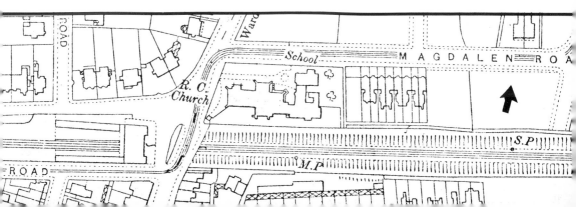

79. Sunday School outings were once a useful additional source of passenger revenue. Here we witness the return of one such trip, behind one of the faithful class E4s, no.32515, on 14th July 1960. The destination was Hailsham – somewhat surprising as the coaches were from the London Midland Region. Maybe they had been borrowed from an overnight train stabled at Eastbourne. (S.C. Nash)

81. The Edwardian architectural extravagance is profuse. In addition to wide passenger ramps and street level gates for parcels to both platforms, a separate ramp for parcels to the down platform was provided. An independent public footbridge across the platforms is still in use. (C. Hall)

80. The position of the signal box is marked S.B. on the map. (W.M. is Weighing Machine). Although photographed in 1975, it remained in use ten years later, controlling semaphore signals. (J. Scrace)

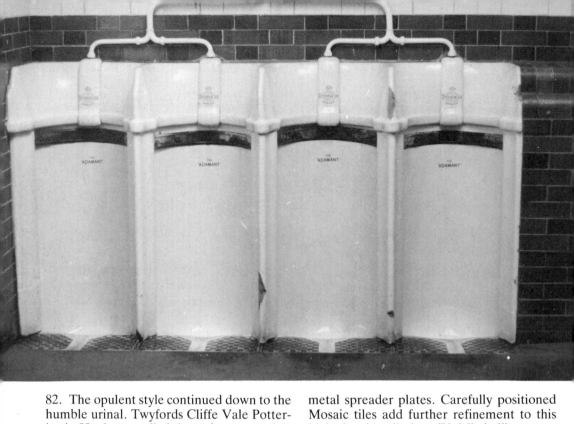

82. The opulent style continued down to the humble urinal. Twyfords Cliffe Vale Potteries in Hanley supplied the *Adamant* models which are still fitted with the now uncommon metal spreader plates. Carefully positioned Mosaic tiles add further refinement to this high-class installation. (V. Mitchell)

The gas works on this 1909 map was that of the Bexhill Water & Gas Co and was in production between 1887 and 1967. The electricity works generated DC current from 1900 until 1955. On the right of the map are the Galley Hill sidings, used mainly for household coal.

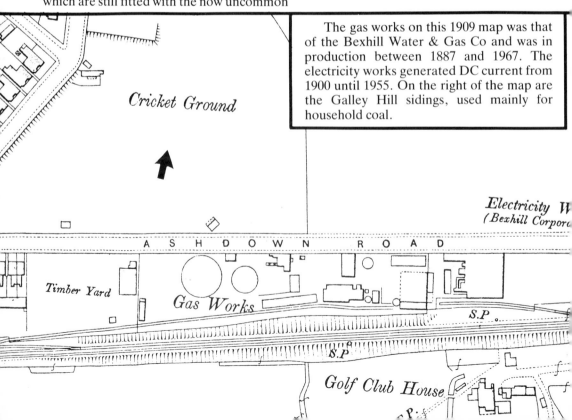

83. A goods loop and five sidings were situated opposite the signal box shown in this 1975 photograph. In 1985, one siding remained in use to serve a domestic oil terminal. (J. Scrace)

Continued overleaf →

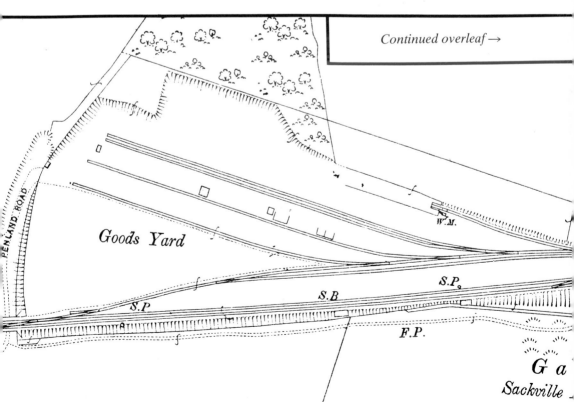

GLYNE GAP HALT

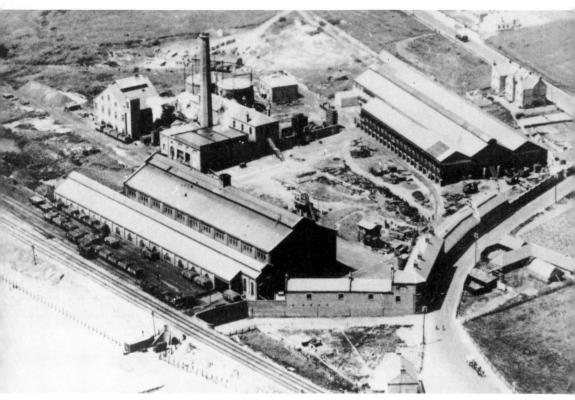

84. An interesting railway feature is a wagon traverser just visible at the end of the four parallel coal sidings and in line with the large opening in the wall of the nearest building, a coal store adjacent to the retort house. The road going from the top to the bottom of the picture is the coast road, now A259. In the centre is the boiler house and engine room and the long buildings on the right housed the gas purifiers. (Hastings Reference Library)

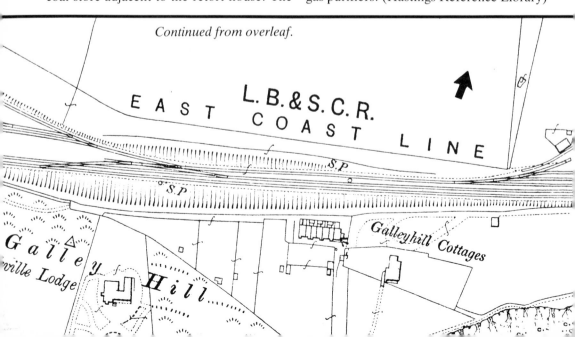

Continued from overleaf.

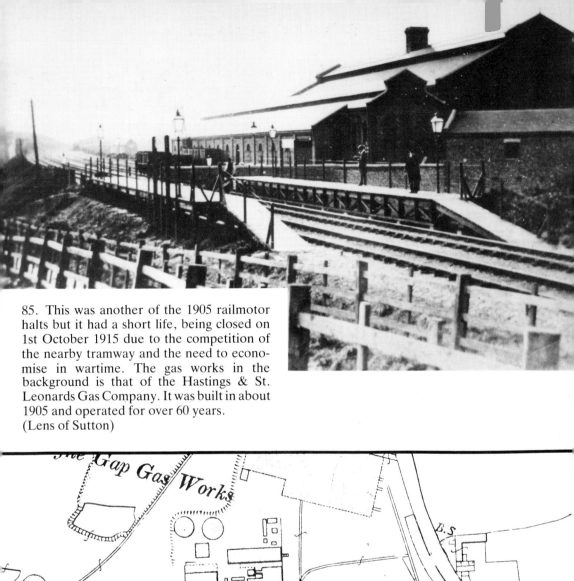

85. This was another of the 1905 railmotor halts but it had a short life, being closed on 1st October 1915 due to the competition of the nearby tramway and the need to economise in wartime. The gas works in the background is that of the Hastings & St. Leonards Gas Company. It was built in about 1905 and operated for over 60 years. (Lens of Sutton)

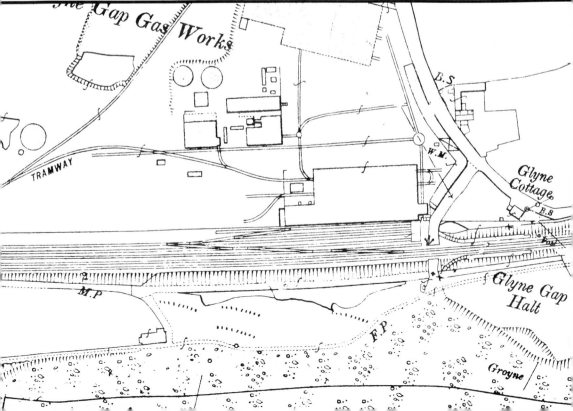

86. Steam railcar no.2 leaves for St. Leonards West Marina. The SECR would not allow railmotors onto their line into Hastings owing, in part, to traffic congestion in the tunnels. This restriction would have been another factor affecting the poor traffic at this halt. The power unit was built by Beyer Peacock and the 48-seat coachwork was by the Electric Railway and Tramway Carriage Works of Preston (Lens of Sutton)

BRIGHTON TO HASTINGS.

STATIONS.	Goods A.M.		Goods A.M.		Passengr A.M.		Parly. A.M.		Passenger A.M.		Passengr P.M.		Passengr P.M.		Goods P.M.		Passengr P.M.		Passenger P.M.			
	arr.	dep.	arr.	dep.	arr.	dep.	arr.	dep.	arr.	dep.	arr.	dep.	arr.	dep.	arr.	dep.	arr.	dep	arr.	dep.	arr.	dep.
Brighton..	...	4 0	...	6 30	...	8 0	...	8 45	...	11 15	...	2 10	...	3 35	...	4 0	...	5 35	...	8 35		
Falmer ...	4 15	4 25	...	6 45	8 11	8 13	8 54	8 55	...	11 27½	19½	20	...	3 45	4 15	4 20	...	5 45	8 47	8 48		
Lewes	4 40	4 50	6 59	7 15	8 25	...	9 5	9 10	11 38	11 40	22	35	...	3 58	4 30	...	5 54	5 55	9 0	9 10		
Glynde ...	5 2	5 12	7 25	7 35	...	...	9 19	9 20	...	11 46	...	...	4 0	4 6	...	...	6 4	6 5	...	9 16		
Berwick...	5 24	5 34	7 50	8 0	...	...	9 29	9 30	11 54	11 55	...	...	4 18	4 14	...	...	6 14	6 15	...	9 24		
Polegate ..	5 50	6 5	8 15	8 25	...	...	9 38	9 40	12 8	12 5	...	...	4 21	4 22	...	...	6 24	6 25	9 28	9 30		
Pevensey..	6 20	6 30	8 40	8 50	...	...	9 49	9 50	12 14	12 15	...	...	4 29	4 30	...	...	6 34	6 35	9 39	9 40		
Bexhill ...	6 45	6 55	9 5	9 15	...	...	9 59	10 0	12 27	12 28	...	...	4 39	4 40	...	...	6 44	6 45	9 49	9 50		
St. Lenrd's	7 7	7 17	9 25	9 30	...	...	10 8	10 10	12 38	12 40	...	...	4 44	4 45	...	...	6 49	6 50	9 53	9 55		
Hastings..	7 30	..	9 45	..	...	...	10 20	..	12 50	...	...	...	6 0	...	...	...	7 0	...	10 0	...		

HASTINGS TO BRIGHTON.

STATIONS.	Parly. A.M.		Passengr. A.M.		Passenger A.M.		Passenger. P.M.		Passengr. P.M.		Goods. P.M.		Passengr. P.M.		Goods. P.M.		Goods. P.M.			
	arr.	dep.	arr.	dep.	arr.	dep.	arr.	dep.	arr.	dep.	arr.	dep.	arr.	dep.	arr.	dep.	arr.	dep.	arr.	dep.
Hastings	...	6 45	...	8 50	...	9 50	...	12 25	...	...	...	3 50	...	5 45	...	...	...	7 0		
St. Leonard's	6 49	6 50	8 54	8 55	9 54	9 55	12 29	12 30	...	...	4 0	4 15	5 49	5 50	...	...	7 13	7 23		
Bexhill	6 55	6 56	...	9 0	10 0	10 1	12 36	12 37	...	...	...	4 25	5 59	6 0	...	...	7 35	7 45		
Pevensey ...	7 10	7 11	...	9 10	10 10	10 11	12 49	12 50	...	...	...	4 45	6 14	6 15	...	...	8 0	8 10		
Polegate ...	7 21	7 21	9 13	9 15	10 20	10 22	12 58	1 0	...	...	4 55	5 5	6 25	6 26	...	...	8 25	8 40		
Berwick....	7 32	7 33	...	9 21	10 31	10 32	1 10	1 11	...	...	5 15	5 25	6 35	6 36	...	...	8 56	9 6		
Glynde	7 42	7 43	...	9 28	10 41	10 42	1 20	1 21	...	...	5 35	5 50	6 45	6 46	...	...	9 18	9 28		
Lewes	7 50	7 55	9 33	9 35	10 48	10 50	1 30	1 35	3 0	6 10	6 20	6 59	7 0	8 18	8 25	9 40	9 55		
Falmer	8 9	8 10	...	9 45	11 4	11 5	...	1 50	...	3 13	...	6 35	7 14	7 15	...	8 45	...	10 15		
Brighton ..	8 25	...	9 55	...	11 20	...	2 5	...	3 25	...	7 0	...	7 30	...	9 0	...	10 30	...		

Two pages from a working timetable (undated) of about 1849

87. Viewed in April 1957, the diesel maintenance and inspection shed had not by then become operational. It is 440ft long and was built partly on land occupied by the Hastings Corporation Yard. Some of the shorter 3-windowed motor coaches were later incorporated into the 'Tadpole' sets used between Tonbridge and Reading. (British Rail)

88. A 750ft long carriage shed for cleaning and berthing the special narrow body stock was erected to the east of the other shed. Looking east from a Hastings-bound train in 1985, we see the connection to the coast line in the foreground and the separate line for empty stock working to the washing plant. This line joins the main line at Bopeep Junction and all were about to be electrified, in readiness for the abolition of the diesel-electrics in May 1986. (V. Mitchell)

ST. LEONARDS WEST
MARINA

89. In addition to the two steam railmotors, two petrol cars, numbered 3 and 4, were built in 1905. Each was fitted with two 4-cylinder Daimler 35hp engines and seats for 48 passengers. The end gates were soon dispensed with and fully glazed ends provided. Their petrol consumption was 5mpg and as their reliability was poor, they were withdrawn in 1908. (R.C. Riley collection)

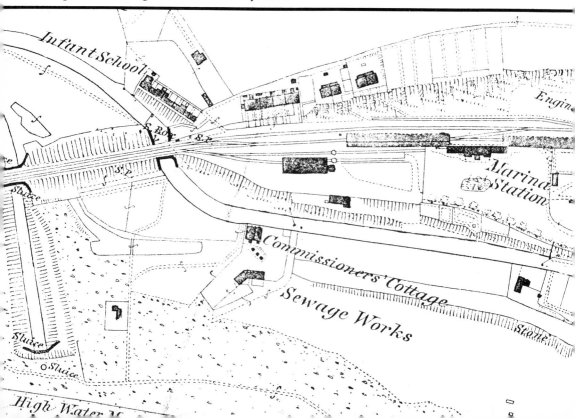

90. This was the most easterly station on the LBSCR system and their track ended at Bopeep Junction. Their locomotive depot was therefore built here, in the cutting on the right. A class D3 waits to leave for Hastings on 23rd October 1934. (H.C. Casserley)

1873 map

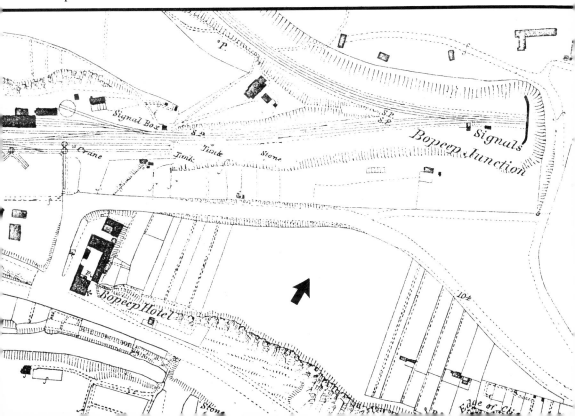

91. Looking east in June 1950, it appears that the down platform canopy has suffered bomb damage and the gas lamp posts still have their wartime white bands. On the right is the former cattle dock. (D. Clayton)

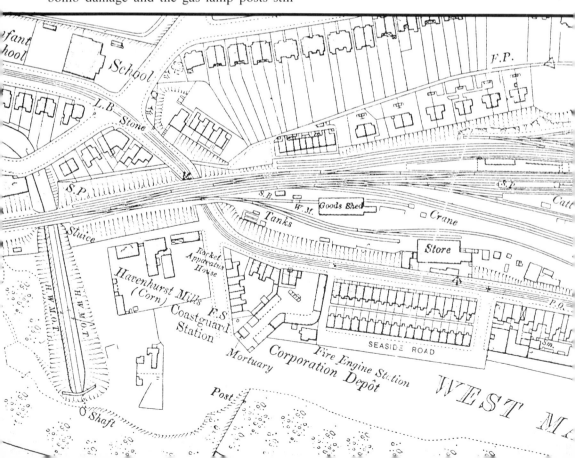

92. An unusual visitor on 31st May 1953 was LMR locomotive no.43404. It is departing with a return excursion to Tring. On the right there was a goods shed and a siding for banana traffic. (S.C. Nash)

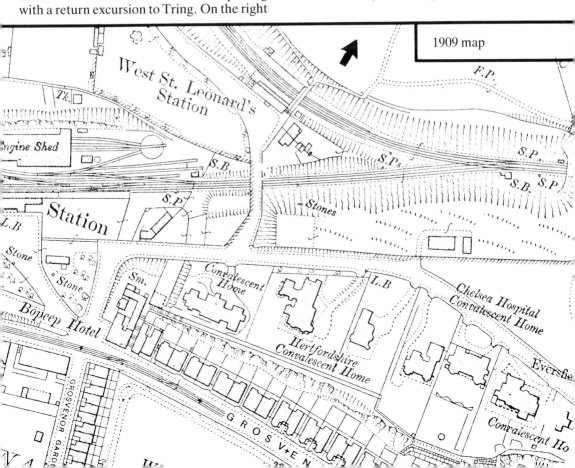

1909 map

93. The station was known as Hastings & St. Leonards until 1851 and plain St. Leonards until 1870. The buildings seen here in 1957 were erected in 1888-89 and were closed to all traffic on 10th July 1967. (D. Cullum)

95. On 11th April 1931, engine nos. A763, A94 and A717 were on shed. The depot reached its zenith between 1929 (when Hastings shed closed) and 1935 (when the coastal electrification took place), although a large fleet of 4–4–0s, particularly 'Schools' class, was allocated here until dieselisation. (H.C. Casserley)

94. The 1873 map shows the original two road engine shed which was replaced in about 1899 with this four road structure. *Gladstone* was built in 1882 at a cost of £2655 and is seen here when last running in umber livery. It was withdrawn in 1927 for preservation and is now shining umber again in the care of the National Railway Museum. (E.R. Lacey collection)

96. A westward view from the road bridge in 1957 shows the coaling crane and the 50ft hand-operated turntable. The track leading onto it in the foreground does not appear on the 1910 map, having been added by the SR to reduce engine movements. (D. Cullum)

———▶

97. Class E4 no.32518 stands by the down platform water column as an up goods train rumbles through on 11th October 1949. 'Schools' class no.30910 *Merchant Taylors* and C class no.31038 blow off ready for work as a driver emerges from the shed. BR provided the new asbestos roof and brick ends. (British Rail)

98. On 23rd April 1958, construction of a carriage washing machine was in progress. This was for use by the new diesel-electric trains. The shed remained in casual use by diesel locomotives for a few years. (British Rail) ———▶

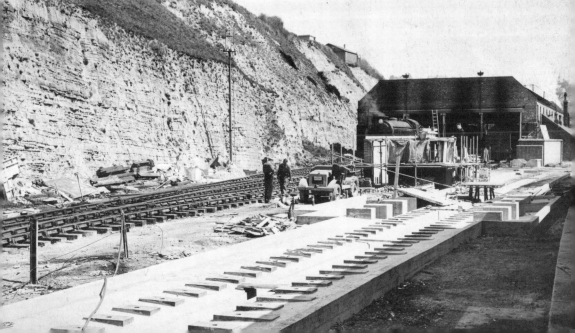

99. Bopeep Junction in 1892. The LBSCR line to Bexhill is on the left and the SER line to Tunbridge Wells curves through West St. Leonards station. Beyond the road bridge is the old engine shed and water tower. The chimney was probably used by a steam-powered water pump. (Lens of Sutton)

100. A class L 4–4–0 emerges from the 1318yd long Bopeep Tunnel with empty stock from Bexhill West bound for West Marina sidings, on 4th June 1950. Since this journey involved reversals at Crowhurst and Hastings, a locomotive was provided at the other end of the train as well. It was class N1 2–6–0 no.31876. (S.C. Nash)

→

101. The 11.34 Brighton to Ore EMU passes Bopeep Junction signal box on 5th June 1975, by which time West Marina station had disappeared. The single non-electrified line under the right hand arch passed through the washing machine and continued onto the carriage sheds. (J. Scrace)

ST. LEONARDS
WARRIOR SQUARE

102. The SECR made it quite clear that it was *their* station, although LBSCR trains did stop there. Even this was not allowed prior to 5th December 1870, the rival's trains being forced to pass through non-stop. The two companies maintained separate booking offices until 1923. (Lens of Sutton)

SOUTH EASTERN RAILWAY.

HASTINGS to
ST. LEONARDS [WARRIOR SQUARE]

Series 3]   Third Class.

St. Leonards   St. Leonards

1148

103. The construction of Bopeep Junction Tunnel presented many problems due to the varied geology and numerous springs. Only a single line was used from about 1885 until 1906 due to reduced clearances. Further reconstruction work took place in 1950. DS1169 stands on the down line on 26th May during a further period of "engineer's possession". (J.J. Smith)

104. Two 2NOL units from Ore to Brighton run "wrong road" on 22nd March 1952, due to permanent way work on the up line in the tunnel. At the end of the platforms is the 788yd Hastings Tunnel. (S.C. Nash)

105. Skilful photography reveals the dignified form of the 1851 station building and house, visible only since the removal of the down platform canopy. The exterior has been enhanced by the loss of an awning. (C. Hall)

NEW THROUGH COASTAL SERVICE

EVERY TUESDAY,

Commencing in JULY, Through Trains, 1st, and 3rd Class will r between the undermentioned Stations at the times shown below, viz.:

LONDON BRIGHTON & SOUTH COAST RAILWAY TO SOUTH EASTERN & CHATHAM RAILWA

OUT.		a.m.		HOME.		p.
Brighton ... ... dep.		9 5		Deal ... ... dep.		5
London Road ... ... ,,		8‡ 59		Walmer ... ... ,,		5
Lewes ... ... ,,		9 21		Dover Harbour.. ... ... ,,		6
*Eastbourne ... ... ,,		9 20	B	Folkestone (Central) ... ... ,,		6
Bexhill ... ... ,,		9 53		Margate Sands§ ... ... ,,		5
St. Leonards (W.M.) ... ... ,,		10 0		Ramsgate Town§ ... ... ,,		5
St. Leonards (Warrior Square) ... ,,		10 5		Canterbury (West)§ ... ... ,,		6
Hastings ... ... arr.		10 8		Ashford ... ... arr.		6
Hastings ... ... dep.		10 25		Ashford ... ... dep.		6
Ashford ... ... arr.		11 5		Hastings ... ... arr.		7
Ashford ... ... dep.		11 9		Hastings ... ... dep.		7
Canterbury (West)§ ... ... arr.		11 33		St. Leonards (Warrior Square) ... ,,		7
Ramsgate Town§ ... ... ,,		12 2		St. Leonards (W.M.) ... ... arr.		7
Margate Sands§ ... ... ,,		12 15		Bexhill ... ... ,,		7
Folkestone (Central) ... ... ,,		11 28		*Eastbourne ... ... ,,		8
Dover Harbour... ... ... ,,		11 43		Lewes ... ... ,,		8
Walmer ... ... ,,		12 1		Brighton ... ... ,,		8
Deal ... ... ,,		12 5				

106. The elegant exterior is just visible – more obvious is the unroofed gentleman's toilet, a design favoured by most railway architects. The station was known as Gensing in its early days. (C. Hall) 1912

OUTH EASTERN & CHATHAM RAILWAY TO LONDON BRIGHTON & SOUTH COAST RAILWA

OUT.						a.m.	HOME.						p.r
ırgate Sands§	...	...	...	...	... dep.	8 40	Brighton ...	...	...	...	...	... dep.	7
ınsgate Town§	...	...	...	...	,,	8 50	Lewes ...	...	...	...	...	,,	7
al	...	...	...	...	,,	8 45	*Eastbourne	...	...	...	,,	7
almer ...	...	...	...	...	,,	8 48	Bexhill	...	...	...	...	,,	8
ver Priory	...	...	...	...	,,	9 6	St. Leonards (W.M.)	...	...	...	,,	8
ver Harbour...	...	...	...	...	,,	9 9	St. Leonards (Warrior Square)	...	...	,,	8
ıkestone (Central)	...	...	...	...	,,	9 24	Hastings ...	...	...	...	... arr.	8
hford	...	...	...	...	... arr.	9 45	Hastings ...	...	...	...	... dep.	8
hford	...	...	...	...	... dep.	9 50	Ashford	...	...	...	... arr.	9
stings	...	...	...	...	... arr.	10 27	Ashford	...	...	...	... dep.	9
stings...	...	...	...	...	... dep.	10 35	Folkestone (Central)	...	...	... arr.	9
Leonards (Warrior Square)	...	...	,,			10 37	Dover Harbour...	...	...	...	,,	10
Leonards (W.M.)...	...	...	... arr.			10 42	Dover Priory	...	...	...	,,	10
xhill	...	...	...	...	,,	10 50	Walmer	...	...	...	...	,,	10
*Eastbourne	...	...	...	,,		11 26	Deal ...	...	...	...	...	,,	10
wes	...	...	...	...	,,	11 38	Ramsgate Town §	...	...	...	,,	10
ighton ...	...	...	...	,,		11 58	Margate Sands §	...	...	...	...	,,	10

B Local Passengers between Brighton, Hastings and intermediate Stations are not conveyed by these trains.
* Eastbourne Passengers change at Polegate.　‡ Change at Lewes.　§ Change at Ashford.
Passengers holding Excursion Tickets are not allowed to take luggage.

EAP TICKETS will be issued between the Principal Coast Towns by these Trains.　*For full particulars see Special*

HASTINGS

107. Before the former SER locomotive shed was closed in 1929, the SR provided a 55ft turntable and a new coal stage. This was close to the east end of Hastings Tunnel and was in use from 1926 to 1957. A driver relaxes and reads his newspaper on 6th June 1950. (D. Clayton)

109. A photograph from about 1910 shows a train departing from platform 2 with another standing in platform 4. Nos. 3 and 4 were added to relieve congestion but did not have any weather protection. Passengers on platform 1 were no doubt admiring Mr. Stirling's class F, standing near the turntable. (P. Hay collection)

108. Another view from Linton Road bridge shows an unusual visitor – the Brighton Belle set no. 3053 on aRCTS railtour on 8th April 1972. (S.C. Nash)

The 1873 map shows the curious V-shaped station which gave one through platform for SER trains and a terminal one for use by LBSCR services. Note the small wagon turntables and lack of houses nearby.

110. Here is another example of the SECR emphasising its ownership of a station. Readers are invited to explain the mysterious aerial objects above the sign so that we can describe them in a future revised edition. (Lens of Sutton)

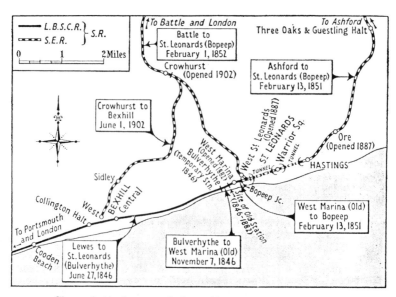

Chronological map of the railways around Hastings

(Railway Magazine)

111. On the left is the three road engine shed of 1852; in the centre are the gas works (which closed in 1907) and the goods shed, and on the right is platform 1.
(Lens of Sutton)

112. The austere platforms 3 and 4 are even devoid of seats. Maybe they were mainly used for the departure of extra trains in the summer. The main attraction to visitors is visible on the skyline – Hastings Castle.
(Lens of Sutton)

LONDON BRIGHTON AND SOUTH COAST
SOUTH EASTERN AND CHATHAM RAILWAYS.

NEW THROUGH COASTAL SERVICE.

EVERY TUESDAY COMMENCING JULY.

Through Trains, 1st and 3rd Class, run between the undermentioned Stations at the times shown below,

VIZ.:—

L. B. & S. C. R. to S. E. & C. R.

OUT.		a.m.	HOME.		p.m.
Brighton ... ... dep.		9 5			
London Road ... ... ,,		8†59	Dover Town ... ... dep.		6 10
Lewes ... ... ,,		9 21	Folkestone (Central) ... ,,		6 24
*Eastbourne ... ... ,,	B	9 20	Margate Sands ... ... ,,		5§40
Bexhill ... ... ,,		9 53	Ramsgate Town ... ... ,,		5§50
St. Leonards (W. Marina) ... ,,		10 0	Walmer ... ... ,,		5§18
St. Leonards (W. Square) ... ,,		10 5	Deal ... ... ,,		5§25
Hastings ... ... arr.		10 8	Canterbury (West) ... ,,		6§18
Hastings ... ... dep.		10 20	Ashford ... ... arr.		6 45
Ashford ... ... arr.		11 0			
Ashford ... ... dep.		11 4	Ashford ... ... dep.		6 50
Canterbury (West) ... ... arr.		11§28	Hastings ... ... arr.		7 30
		p.m.	Hastings ... ... dep.		7 43
Deal ... ... ,,		12§6	St. Leonards (W. Square) ... arr.		7 46
Walmer ... ... ,,		12§12	St. Leonards (W. Marina) ... ,,		7 51
Ramsgate Town ... ... ,,		12§2	Bexhill ... ... ,,	B	7 59
Margate Sands ... ... ,,		12§15	*Eastbourne ... ... ,,		8 34
		a.m.	Lewes ... ... ,,		8 35
Folkestone (Central) ... ,,		11 23	London Road ... ... ,,		9 12
Dover Town ... ... ,,		11 36	Brighton ... ... ,,		8 53

S. E. & C. R. to L. B. & S. C. R.

OUT.	a.m.	HOME.	p.m.
Margate Sands ... ... dep.	8§40	Brighton ... ... dep.	7 15
Ramsgate Town ... ... ,,	8§50	Lewes ... ... ,,	7 33
Deal ... ... ,,	8ᴅ32	*Eastbourne ... ... ,,	7 30
Walmer ... ... ,,	8ᴅ37	Bexhill ... ... ,,	8 14
Dover Priory ... ... ,,	9 6	St. Leonards (W. Marina) ... ,,	8 21
Dover Harbour ... ... ,,	9 9	St. Leonards (W. Square) ... ,,	8 26
Folkestone (Central) ... ,,	9 24	Hastings ... ... arr.	8 30
Ashford ... ... arr.	9 40	Hastings ... ... dep.	8 40
Ashford ... ... dep.	9 45	Ashford ... ... arr.	9 23
Hastings ... ... arr.	10 27	Ashford ... ... dep.	9 35
Hastings ... ... dep.	10 35	Folkestone (Central) ... arr.	10 11
St. Leonards (W. Square) ... arr.	10 37	Dover Harbour ... ... ,,	10 27
St. Leonards (W. Marina) ... ,,	10 42	Dover Priory ... ... ,,	10 32
Bexhill ... ... ,,	10 50	Deal ... ... ,,	10§37
*Eastbourne ... ... ,,	11 27	Walmer ... ... ,,	10§42
Lewes ... ... ,,	11 38	Ramsgate Town ... ... ,,	10§27
Brighton ... ... ,,	11 58	Margate Sands ... ... ,,	10§40

RETURN FARES by these Special Trains in either direction.

To and From	To and From Brighton and London Road.		To and From Lewes.		To and From Eastbourne.		To and From Bexhill.		To and From St. Leonards.	
	1	3	1	3	1	3	1	3	1	3
	s. d.	s. d.	s. d.	s. d.	s. d.	s. d.	s. d.	s. d.	s. d.	s. d.
Margate	15 4	8 6	14 1	7 6	12 8	6 4	10 9	5 0	10 4	4 8
Ramsgate Town										
Deal	14 10	8 6	13 7	7 6	12 2	6 4	10 3	5 0	9 10	4 8
Walmer										
Dover	13 4	8 0	12 1	7 0	10 8	5 10	8 9	4 6	8 4	4 2
Folkestone Central	12 6	7 6	10 11	6 6	9 6	5 4	7 7	4 0	7 2	3 8
†Canterbury	12 2	7 6	10 11	6 6	9 6	5 4	7 7	4 0	7 2	3 8
Ashford	10 4	6 9	9 1	5 9	7 8	4 7	5 9	3 3	5 4	2 11

B—Local Passengers between Brighton, Hastings and intermediate Stations are not conveyed by this Train
D—Change at Dover Harbour.
† Passengers are booked from L.B. & S.C.R. Stations to Canterbury, but not *vice versa*.
* Eastbourne Passengers change at Polegate.   ‡ Change at Lewes.   § Change at Ashford.
Tickets available on the day of issue only.
Local and Through Tickets at ordinary fares are also available by these Trains. Passengers holding
Excursion Tickets are not allowed to take luggage with them.

113. The entire station was rebuilt in 1931, only the goods shed remaining unaltered. A notably spacious booking hall was provided in this neo-Georgian style building, photographed soon after completion. (N. Langridge collection)

114. Two island platforms were provided in the new layout, the left hand one being on the site of the former locomotive depot. Two points of interest to look for – first, the lengthy inspection pit on the left and, second, the post office building being erected on the right. (D. Cullum collection)

115. The goods yard had a fan of twelve sidings as well as two to a dock and a crane. The new covered footbridge was of generous width to reduce crowding at busy times. (D. Cullum collection)

London Brighton and South Coast Railway

Hastings to

Shoreham

116. In the 1950s, Hastings was the destination for a number of summer services from the Midlands and the North. This is the overnight train from Manchester arriving on 16th August 1958, having been hauled from Eastbourne by K class no. 32345. (J.J. Smith)

117. The low morning sun perfectly illuminates the running gear of class U1 no. 31910 as it arrives with the 5.45am from London Bridge on 3rd October 1959. (S.C. Nash)

118. On 19th September 1964, this Terrier made its last journey on BR, from Eastbourne MPD to Robertsbridge reversing at Hastings. It now operates on the Kent & East Sussex Railway as no. 10 *Sutton*, an outline of its unusual history appearing in our *Branch Line to Hayling* under its original number of 50 and several photographs of it are included in our *Branch Line to Tenterden*. (S.C. Nash)

119. Whilst a London train stands in platform 4 on 5th June 1982, no. 33212 removes a defective 3D unit to St. Leonards depot. The middle coach is close to the site of the former West Box. (S.C. Nash)

120. All four platform roads are signalled for reversible running, giving great operating flexibility. The line on the right has long been known as 'Brighton siding', maintaining a link with the station's past. A Victoria train is signalled away by colour light signals in September 1984, whilst the Charing Cross service waits behind semaphores. (C. Wilson)

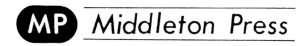

MP Middleton Press

Easebourne Lane, Midhurst, West Sussex, GU29 9AZ
☎ Midhurst (073 081) 3169

BRANCH LINES
BRANCH LINES TO MIDHURST	0 906520 01 0
BRANCH LINES TO HORSHAM	0 906520 02 9
BRANCH LINE TO SELSEY	0 906520 04 5
BRANCH LINES TO EAST GRINSTEAD	0 906520 07 X
BRANCH LINES TO ALTON	0 906520 11 8
BRANCH LINE TO HAYLING	0 906520 12 6
BRANCH LINE TO SOUTHWOLD	0 906520 15 0
BRANCH LINE TO TENTERDEN	0 906520 21 5
BRANCH LINES TO NEWPORT	0 906520 26 6

SOUTH COAST RAILWAYS
BRIGHTON TO WORTHING	0 906520 03 7
WORTHING TO CHICHESTER	0 906520 06 1
CHICHESTER TO PORTSMOUTH	0 906520 14 2
BRIGHTON TO EASTBOURNE	0 906520 16 9
RYDE TO VENTNOR	0 906520 19 3
EASTBOURNE TO HASTINGS	0 906520 27 4

SOUTHERN MAIN LINES
WOKING TO PORTSMOUTH	0 906520 25 8
HAYWARDS HEATH TO SEAFORD	0 906520 28 2

STEAMING THROUGH
STEAMING THROUGH KENT	0 906520 13 4
STEAMING THROUGH EAST HANTS	0 906520 18 5
STEAMING THROUGH EAST SUSSEX	0 906520 22 3

OTHER RAILWAY BOOKS
INDUSTRIAL RAILWAYS OF THE SOUTH-EAST	0 906520 09 6
WAR ON THE LINE The official history of the SR in World War II	0 906520 10 X
GARRAWAY FATHER AND SON The story of two careers in steam	0 906520 20 7

OTHER BOOKS
MIDHURST TOWN – THEN & NOW	0 906520 05 3
EAST GRINSTEAD – THEN & NOW	0 906520 17 7
THE GREEN ROOF OF SUSSEX A refreshing amble along the South Downs Way	0 906520 08 8
THE MILITARY DEFENCE OF WEST SUSSEX	0 906520 23 1
WEST SUSSEX WATERWAYS	0 906520 24 X
BATTLE OVER PORTSMOUTH A City at war in 1940	0 906520 29 0